100 Lifelong Words

Helping Students
Become Better Spellers

by Darlene Mannix

Good Apple
A Division of Frank Schaffer Publications

Editorial Director: Kristin Eclov

Editor: Concetta Doti Ryan, M.A.

Illustrator: Cary Pillo

Inside Design: Shelly Brown

Cover Design: Shelly Brown

Cover Illustration: Cary Pillo

Good Apple
A Division of Frank Schaffer Publications, Inc.
23740 Hawthorne Boulevard
Torrance, CA 90505

Table of Contents

Introduction

This resource book is a collection of activities intended to give students multiple opportunities to recognize, read, write, and use high-frequency words that are often misspelled. These are words which are commonly confused, follow no phonetic rules, or are simply difficult to spell. Because the words are high-frequency, the term "lifelong" is used to indicate that the words should be learned and committed to memory for one's entire life! These are words that students will use again and again.

The pool of 100 words was selected from lists of words that are commonly misspelled by elementary writers. Although the lessons are organized in alphabetical order, the words themselves and the activities can be used in many different ways according to the needs of the individual learners. The following list describes the types of activities you will find in this book.

▲ **Identify the lifelong word in context.**
Students will read the sample sentences and circle the lifelong word in each sentence. Students practice both reading and spelling skills in this activity.

▲ **Write the lifelong word five times.**
A reproducible activity sheet is provided on page 106. Students can use this page to write each word five times.

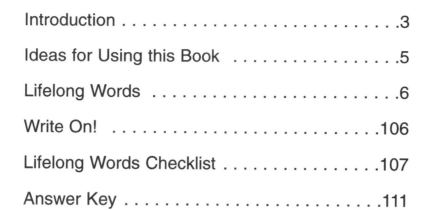

▲ **Recognize and identify the correct spelling of the lifelong word.** There are many incorrect or "decoy" words, so students must look carefully to find the examples that are spelled correctly. Then, students must write the number of times that the word was spelled correctly.

▲ **Write the lifelong word letter by letter, emphasizing the correct sequence of letters.**

▲ **Unscramble the letters of the lifelong word by writing the number that indicates the sequence of letters.** In this way, students do not just write the word because they know what it is, but rather, they must pay close attention to the order of the letters.

▲ **Use the lifelong word to fill in the blanks in a sentence.** The sentences also have blanks for words other than the lifelong word, which requires students to read sentences carefully.

▲ **Answer questions using complete sentences.** The questions are geared so that a response must be written using the lifelong word.

▲ **Identify small words that are contained within the lifelong word.** Students are encouraged to make a list of words using the letters and then write down how many words were made.

▲ **Write complete sentences to answer a question or describe a picture which involves the lifelong word.**

▲ **Locate and identify the lifelong word five times in a word search.**

By using multiple approaches to learning a word, students have many opportunities to commit the spelling of the words to memory.

Ideas for Using this Book

The materials in this book can be used in many different ways to help teach mastery of commonly misspelled words. Some of these ideas are listed below:

▲ **Extra Practice!** Some students need to spend more time (in different ways) working with difficult words. Repetition or repeated writing alone will not necessarily work with these students, but using the words in different ways will provide more opportunities for students to practice the words, and a greater likelihood that the words will be committed to memory.

▲ **Individualization!** A student may be a good speller in general, but may have difficulty with a few tricky words. The teacher can pull out the activities for selected words and have individual students work through "their" difficult words.

▲ **Word of the Week!** Focus on one word each week, and everyone in the class must learn how to spell it. Write the lifelong words 3" x 5" (7.5 cm x 12.5 cm) index cards. Placing the cards on a "word wall" as they are learned, can visually demonstrate the progress of the class.

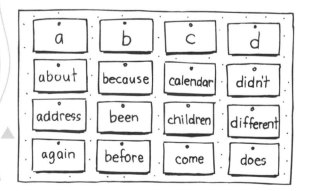

▲ **Generalization!** After focusing on a lifelong word, the teacher may insist that the word can no longer be misspelled on ANY form of writing—social studies, science, even math! Have students look through their writing in all subjects, not just spelling, to find evidence that they are using the lifelong words correctly.

▲ **Seatwork!** Ever have a few minutes that need to be filled? These activities can be used as creative seatwork or independent learning for students who have a few minutes now and then. Once the instructions are learned, the activities can easily be completed independently.

▲ **Spelling Lists or Bonus Words!** A teacher can add a lifelong word or two to the regular weekly spelling list. The lifelong word may be a "bonus" word. Perhaps one week each month could serve as lifelong word week, with all spelling words consisting of these high-frequency words.

▲ **Incentive!** Teachers can offer an appropriate prize to anyone in the class who accepts the challenge of spelling all 100 lifelong words correctly.

▲ **Lifelong Word Spelling Bee!** Students love the challenge of a spelling bee. Use the lifelong words as your word list.

Name _____

about

1. Circle the word **about** in the sentences.

   I think it is about midnight.

   Do you ever wonder about if there is life on other planets?

   I am looking for a book about endangered animals.

2. Fill in the blanks. Use the lifelong word where it is appropriate.

   We were _____ to win the game, but then it started to rain.

   What happened at the game?

   We were _____ to win the game, but then it started to _____.

   I want to see a movie _____ spiders.

   What do I want to see?

   I want to _____ a movie _____ spiders.

   This car is just _____ out of gas.

   What is wrong with this car?

   This _____ is just _____ out of gas.

3. Find the word **about** five times.

i	h	d	r	o	b	c	y	a	k	b
f	k	a	b	o	u	t	m	a	n	n
t	a	s	a	s	a	b	o	u	t	a
r	l	k	b	h	u	l	t	f	n	b
b	c	d	o	p	q	s	l	f	z	o
x	m	t	u	l	a	f	h	e	a	u
d	e	e	t	v	j	a	b	o	u	t

Name_____

1. Circle the word **address** in the sentences.

   Write your address on this piece of paper.
   What is the address of your school?
   My address is 207 East Fifth Street.

   Mr. Bob Smith
   430 Elm Street
   Anywhere, CA
   90000

2. Write the word **address** five times.

   _____ _____ _____

   _____ _____

3. Circle the correct spelling of the word **address**.
   Put an X on the words that are not correct.

   address   adress   addres   address   adddress   adriss
   uddress   address   adress   address   address   adress

   How many correct words did you find? _____

4. Write the word **address** letter by letter.

   a

Name_____

again

1. Circle the word **again** in the sentences.

   That game was fun! Let's play it again.

   Tell me again what you want for your birthday.

   My answer was wrong, so I had to work the problem again.

2. Circle the correct spelling of the word **again**.
   Put an X on the words that are not correct.

agin	again	agian	again	again	aggain
again	aqain	agan	agin	again	agian

   How many correct words did you find? _____

3. How many small words can you make using the letters in **again**?

   _____

   _____

   How many words did you make? _____

4. Fill in the blanks. Use the lifelong word where it is appropriate.

   Please come over to my house _____.

   Where should I go?

   Come to my house _____.

   Let's go for a walk _____ tomorrow.

   When should we go for a walk?

   Let's _____ for a walk _____.

   I like playing ball with you. Let's do it _____.

   What should we do?

   Let's play _____.

a lot

1. Circle the words **a lot** in the sentences.

   Bob wanted to eat a lot of popcorn.
   We will have a lot of fun at the party.
   I think about horses a lot.

2. Write the words **a lot** five times.

   _____   _____   _____

   _____   _____

3. Circle the correct spelling of the words **a lot**.
   Put an X on the words that are not correct.

a lot	alot	alott	alott	a lot	a lot
a lot	a lot	allot	alott	a lot	a lot

   How many correct words did you find? _____

4. Fill in the blanks. Use the lifelong word where it is appropriate.

   Jose wanted to invite _____ of his friends to the game.

   Who did he want to invite to the game?

   Jose wanted to invite _____ of his _____ to the game.

   You might get sick if you eat _____ of cake.

   What will make you sick?

   You might get _____ if you eat _____ of cake.

   Sandy couldn't play because she had _____ of homework.

   Why couldn't Sandy play?

   Sandy couldn't play because she had _____ of _____.

although

1. Circle the word **although** in the sentences.

   Amy and Pete went for a walk, although it was raining outside.

   I only got a C on the test, although I studied hard for it.

   Tony ate his vegetables, although he really didn't like them.

2. Circle the correct spelling of the word **although**.
   Put an X on the words that are not correct.

   allthough   although   allthrough   although   althought   although

   although   althuogh   although   all though   although   altough

   How many correct words did you find? _____

3. How many small words can you make using the letters in **although**?

   _____

   _____

   How many words did you make? _____

4. Fill in the blanks. Use the lifelong word where it is appropriate.

   Fred danced with his cousin at the wedding, _____ he really didn't
   want to.

   Who didn't Fred want to dance with?

   Fred danced with his _____ at the wedding, _____
   he didn't want to.

   Andrea went outside without her coat, _____ it was snowing.

   What did Andrea go outside without?

   Andrea went outside without her _____,
   _____ it was snowing.

   I rode my bike, _____ one of the tires was flat.

   What was wrong with one of the tires?

   I rode my bike, _____ one of the tires was _____.

Name_____

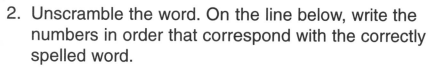

always

1. Circle the word **always** in the sentences.

   Jamal always wears his glasses at school.

   Mrs. Jones always wears her seat belt in the car.

   My family always watches television together
   on Monday night.

2. Unscramble the word. On the line below, write the
   numbers in order that correspond with the correctly
   spelled word.

a	a	w	s	l	y
1	2	3	4	5	6

   _____

3. How many small words can you make using the letters in **always**?

   _____

   _____

   How many words did you make? _____

4. Find the word **always** five times.

a	l	w	a	y	s	a	k	i	m	x
t	o	a	h	f	o	l	m	q	r	t
h	o	l	m	a	l	w	a	y	s	u
f	o	w	g	t	h	a	o	u	c	m
f	r	a	j	o	m	y	h	t	w	n
q	f	y	c	t	e	s	m	h	s	p
x	z	s	a	l	w	a	y	s	x	r

Name_____

around

1. Circle the word **around** in the sentences.

   Put this collar around the dog's neck.

   Let's run around the block.

   Do you think this belt will fit around my waist?

2. Unscramble the word. On the line below, write the
   numbers in order that correspond with the
   correctly spelled word.

d	a	o	r	u	n
1	2	3	4	5	6

   _____

3. Find the word **around** five times.

a	r	o	u	n	d	x	t	h	m	i
x	a	t	s	m	d	m	o	l	f	a
l	r	m	a	n	t	f	t	g	m	r
o	o	a	r	o	u	n	d	g	h	o
q	w	e	t	s	m	o	h	x	e	u
a	r	o	u	n	d	h	m	i	l	n
s	c	w	p	a	r	o	u	n	d	d

because

1. Circle the word **because** in the sentences.

   You should eat vegetables because they are good for you.
   I can't play right now because I have homework to do.
   The team lost the game because they didn't practice.

2. Write the word **because** five times.

   _____   _____   _____

   _____   _____

3. Circle the correct spelling of the word **because**.
   Put an X on the words that are not correct.

   becuse   becouse   because   beuacse   because   bekause

   because   because   beusce   becose   becouse   because

   How many correct words did you find? _____

4. Write the word **because** letter by letter.

   (b)

Name_____

been

1. Circle the word **been** in the sentences.

   My mother asked, "Where have you been?"

   My family has never been to France.

   Sally has been a member of the club for a year.

2. Circle the correct spelling of the word **been**.
   Put an X on the words that are not correct.

ben	been	bene	been	bin	been
been	ben	beene	benn	been	been

   How many correct words did you find? _____

3. How many small words can you make using the letters in **been**?

   _____

   _____

   How many words did you make? _____

4. Fill in the blanks. Use the lifelong word where it is appropriate.

   Since our class has _____ so good, our teacher let us have a free day.

   Why did we get a free day?

   We got a _____ day because our class has _____ so good.

   Maria has _____ a Girl Scout for two years.

   How long has Maria been a Girl Scout?

   Maria has _____ a Girl Scout for _____ years.

   My uncle has _____ in an airplane a lot, because he is a pilot.

   Why has my uncle been in an airplane so much?

   He has _____ in an airplane because he is a _____.

Name _____

before

1. Circle the word **before** in the sentences.

   We better go home before we get in trouble.

   Wipe your feet before you come into the house.

   We only have ten minutes before we have to go.

2. Unscramble the word. On the line below, write
   the numbers in order that correspond with
   the correctly spelled word.

f	e	r	o	e	b
1	2	3	4	5	6

   _____

3. Find the word **before** five times.

b	u	t	b	m	x	t	q	t	r	m
e	r	b	e	o	m	x	a	h	b	l
f	b	e	f	o	r	e	c	q	t	w
o	x	f	o	q	e	c	e	m	d	p
r	m	o	r	h	s	t	f	r	l	s
e	o	r	e	h	x	k	g	u	j	o
t	b	e	f	o	r	e	n	x	k	v

Name_____

birthday

1. Circle the word **birthday** in the sentences.

   Let's wish Tony a happy birthday!
   We are going to a surprise birthday party.
   On my next birthday, I will be 14 years old.

2. How many small words can you make using the letters in **birthday**?

   _____

   _____

   How many words did you make? _____

3. Use the word **birthday** to describe the following picture. Use complete sentences.

_____

_____

_____

_____

Name_____

bought

1. Circle the word **bought** in the sentences.

   Yesterday I bought a new puppy.

   My mother bought a brand-new car.

   We bought a lot of food for the party.

2. Write the word **bought** five times.

   _____   _____   _____

   _____   _____

3. Circle the correct spelling of the word **bought**.
   Put an X on the words that are not correct.

boght	bought	brought	bought	bougt	bought
bought	baught	bought	bot	boughl	baought

   How many correct words did you find? _____

4. Write the word **bought** letter by letter.

   b

busy

1. Circle the word **busy** in the sentences.

   Be careful when you cross the busy street.

   I am too busy to help you with the puzzle now.

   All of this homework will really keep me busy.

2. Circle the correct spelling of the word **busy**.
   Put an X on the words that are not correct.

bussy	busy	buzy	bizzy	busy	busy
busy	bussy	bezy	bussy	busy	busy

   How many correct words did you find? _____

3. How many small words can you make using the letters in **busy**?

   _____

   _____

   How many words did you make? _____

4. Fill in the blanks. Use the lifelong word where it is appropriate.

   Shurae was very _____, so she didn't call me back.

   Why didn't Shurae call me back?

   Shurae didn't call me _____ because she was very _____.

   If the teacher isn't too _____, maybe she will help me draw a picture.

   What would you like the teacher to do?

   I would like the teacher to help me _____ a picture if she isn't too
   _____.

   It's hard to go shopping when the store is _____.

   When is it hard to go shopping?

   When the store is _____, it's hard to go _____.

Name _____

1. Circle the word **calendar** in the sentences.

   At the end of the year, we have to put up a new calendar.

   I have a nice calendar with pictures of animals on it.

   A small calendar can fit into a purse or wallet.

2. Unscramble the word. On the line below, write the numbers in order that correspond with the correctly spelled word.

   a   a   l   r   d   c   n   e
   1   2   3   4   5   6   7   8

   _____

3. Draw a calendar picture for the month of your birthday.

Name_____

children

1. Circle the word **children** in the sentences.

   There were a lot of children at the birthday party.
   My mother had five children.
   Children like to play with toys.

2. Write the word **children** five times.

   _____   _____   _____

   _____   _____

3. Use the word **children** to describe the following picture. Use complete sentences.

   _____

   _____

   _____

   _____

Name_____

come

1. Circle the word **come** in the sentences.

   Call the dog so he will come.

   I want you to come over to my house.

   The little girl wants her birthday to come faster.

2. Unscramble the word. On the line below, write the numbers in order that correspond with the correctly spelled word.

o	e	m	c
1	2	3	4

   _____

3. Find the word **come** five times.

f	l	c	o	m	e	h	l	t	b	x
q	e	c	h	c	o	m	e	l	t	n
t	h	e	c	l	q	e	c	h	z	x
o	f	r	o	b	i	l	h	o	p	r
m	t	m	m	q	e	c	l	m	n	x
c	a	l	e	c	o	m	e	t	c	d
c	o	m	e	l	o	m	s	r	j	j

Name_____

coming

1. Circle the word **coming** in the sentences.

   My favorite uncle is coming for the holidays.
   Amy and I are coming to your house tonight.
   A snowstorm is coming our way.

2. Write the word **coming** five times.

   _____   _____   _____

   _____   _____

3. Circle the correct spelling of the word **coming**.
   Put an X on the words that are not correct.

   comming   coming   comeing   coming   cuming   coming
   coming   coming   coming   cuming   comming   comeing

   How many correct words did you find? _____

4. Write the word **coming** letter by letter.

Name_____

1. Circle the word **could** in the sentences.

   Do you think you could run faster than me?

   If we had some money, we could go to the movies.

   We could go for a walk if it stops raining.

2. Circle the correct spelling of the word **could**.
   Put an X on the words that are not correct.

cold	could	coulld	cud	could	coud
could	cauld	could	colld	could	cowld

   How many correct words did you find? _____

3. How many small words can you make using the letters in **could**?

   _____

   _____

   How many words did you make? _____

4. Fill in the blanks. Use the lifelong word where it is appropriate.

   I _____ get 100% on my test if I study.

   How could I get 100% on my test?

   If I _____, I _____ get 100% on my test.

   None of the cats _____ climb the tree.

   What couldn't climb the tree?

   None of the cats _____ climb the _____.

   Bobby wished that he _____ go to the Water Park.

   What did Bobby want to do?

   Bobby _____ that he _____ go to the Water Park.

Name_____

1. Circle the word **couldn't** in the sentences.

   My family couldn't go to the school play.

   I couldn't make a basket, no matter how hard I tried.

   My dog is black, so that couldn't be him.

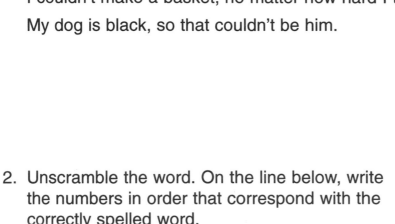

2. Unscramble the word. On the line below, write the numbers in order that correspond with the correctly spelled word.

d	'	t	o	c	l	u	n
1	2	3	4	5	6	7	8

   _____

3. Find the word **couldn't** five times.

f	c	o	u	l	d	n	t	t	s	r
t	o	m	l	o	q	p	n	t	x	x
f	u	c	o	u	l	d	n	t	k	l
r	l	b	r	i	l	e	n	t	c	g
l	d	p	m	u	o	d	e	b	l	p
l	n	l	o	q	u	t	r	e	f	h
f	t	c	a	c	o	u	l	n	d	t

Name_____

1. Circle the word **didn't** in the sentences.

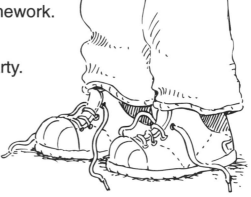

The boy got in trouble because he didn't do his homework.

I didn't tie my shoes, so I fell down.

Anna didn't know that she was having a surprise party.

2. Write the word **didn't** five times.

_____   _____   _____

_____   _____

3. Circle the correct spelling of the word **didn't**.
   Put an X on the words that are not correct.

didnt	didn't	diddn't	did'nt	didn't	didn't
didn't	didn't	dodn't	didn't	didn't	didn't

How many correct words did you find? _____

4. Write the word **didn't** letter by letter.

Name_____

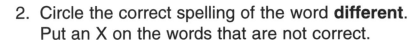

1. Circle the word **different** in the sentences.

   I don't like this sweater, so I will get a different one.

   Have you ever lived in a different city?

   Susanna enjoyed wearing clothes that are different colors.

2. Circle the correct spelling of the word **different**.
   Put an X on the words that are not correct.

   diferent   differant   different   diferrent   different   diffferent

   different   different   deferrent   different   different   differint

   How many correct words did you find? _____

3. Fill in the blanks. Use the lifelong word where it is appropriate.

   We didn't want to get another cat, so we decided to get a
   _____ pet.

   What pet didn't we want to get?

   We didn't want another _____, so we decided to get a
   _____ pet.

   I wish I had a _____bike.

   What do I wish I had?

   I wish I had a _____ bike.

   My father drove up in a _____ car, so I didn't realize it was him.

   Why didn't I realize that my father was driving up?

   My _____ was driving a _____ car.

Name _____

1. Circle the word **does** in the sentences.

    My sister always does the dishes at home.

    What does your best friend like to do on the weekends?

    My dog does a lot of tricks.

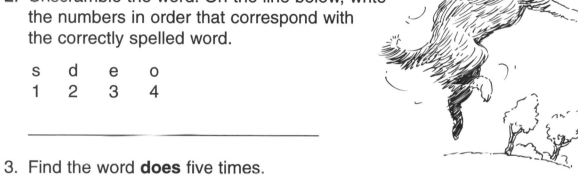

2. Unscramble the word. On the line below, write the numbers in order that correspond with the correctly spelled word.

    s   d   e   o
    1   2   3   4

    _____

3. Find the word **does** five times.

f	d	o	e	s	l	a	a	c	x	v
d	o	e	s	c	o	r	j	u	e	l
h	l	m	o	h	t	d	s	b	i	t
d	m	a	q	r	s	o	u	k	f	m
o	m	d	o	e	s	e	c	p	g	v
e	o	l	m	t	h	s	n	d	o	w
s	s	o	m	i	r	e	c	r	h	q	z

doesn't

1. Circle the word **doesn't** in the sentences.

   My brother doesn't like green beans.

   The dog doesn't want to run after the ball.

   It doesn't look like it will rain today.

2. Write the word **doesn't** five times.

   _____   _____   _____

   _____   _____

3. Circle the correct spelling of the word **doesn't**.
   Put an X on the words that are not correct.

duesn't	doesnt	doesn't	dosen't	doesn't	dosn't
doesn't	dozn't	doesn't	doesn't	does't	does'nt

   How many correct words did you find? _____

4. Write the word **doesn't** letter by letter.

   ⓓ

done

1. Circle the word **done** in the sentences.

   Are you done with your painting?

   My aunt gets her hair done on Saturdays.

   Are you done with that book yet?

2. Write the word **done** five times.

   _____   _____   _____

   _____   _____

3. Circle the correct spelling of the word **done**.
   Put an X on the words that are not correct.

done	donne	dun	don	done	dune
donne	bone	doune	done	done	dune

   How many correct words did you find? _____

4. Unscramble the word. On the line below, write the numbers in order that correspond with the correctly spelled word.

e	o	n	d
1	2	3	4

   _____

5. Write the word **done** letter by letter.

   d

early

1. Circle the word **early** in the sentences.

   My dad leaves early for work.

   Reba turned in her report to the teacher early.

   Children like to get up early on Christmas morning.

2. Circle the correct spelling of the word **early**.
   Put an X on the words that are not correct.

   early   early   erly   irely   early   aerly

   early   errly   early   early   earlly   early

   How many correct words did you find? _____

3. How many small words can you make using the letters in **early**?

   _____

   _____

   How many words did you make? _____

4. Fill in the blanks. Use the lifelong word where it is appropriate.

   The _____ bird gets the worm.

   What does the early bird get?

   The _____ bird gets the _____.

   I don't like to get up _____ on Saturdays.

   When don't I like to get up early?

   I don't _____ to get up _____ on _____.

   We got in line _____ to get tickets for the movie.

   What did we get tickets for?

   We got in line _____ to get _____ for the movie.

Name_____

1. Circle the word **easy** in the sentences.

   This book is too easy for me.

   It is not easy to lift the big stones.

   I am going to take it easy this weekend.

2. Unscramble the word. On the line below, write the numbers in order that correspond with the correctly spelled word.

y	s	a	e
1	2	3	4

   _____

3. Find the word **easy** five times.

o	p	m	c	h	e	a	s	y	z	x
l	t	e	m	l	c	r	o	g	e	v
r	c	a	h	m	l	e	o	e	a	b
l	a	s	m	i	c	a	o	t	s	d
g	r	y	o	c	m	s	t	q	y	n
z	e	a	s	y	t	y	m	r	w	r
o	l	m	n	o	c	h	w	e	z	q

enough

1. Circle the word **enough** in the sentences.

   I have had enough to eat, so don't put any more food on my plate.

   Will we have enough time to finish our game before we have to go?

   I am not tall enough to go on the roller coaster.

2. Fill in the blanks. Use the lifelong word where it is appropriate.

   Lewis didn't have _____ money to buy the sled.

   Why couldn't Lewis buy the sled?

   Lewis didn't have _____ money to _____ the sled.

   My mother has _____ butter to make the cookies.

   What does my mother have enough of?

   She has _____ butter to make _____.

   I don't have _____ time to walk to the store.

   What don't I have enough time to do?

   I don't have _____ time to walk to the _____.

3. Write the word **enough** letter by letter.

   _____

   _____ _____

   _____ _____ _____

   _____ _____ _____ _____

   _____ _____ _____ _____ _____

   e   _____ _____ _____ _____ _____ _____

Name_____

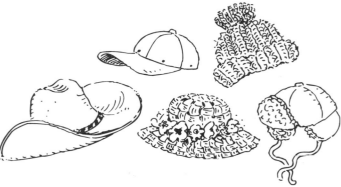

1. Circle the word **every** in the sentences.

   Every person in the room had a hat on.
   I ate every piece of food on my plate.
   We have art every Friday.

2. Write the word **every** five times.

   _____   _____   _____

   _____   _____

3. Circle the correct spelling of the word **every**.
   Put an X on the words that are not correct.

   every   evvery   every   everry   avery   every
   evry   every   every   avery   ivery   evvery

   How many correct words did you find? _____

4. Unscramble the word. On the line below, write the numbers in order that correspond
   with the correctly spelled word.

   y   e   e   v   r
   1   2   3   4   5

   _____

5. Write the word **every** letter by letter.

everybody

1. Circle the word **everybody** in the sentences.

   The teacher told everybody to sit down.

   Everybody in the room was wearing a hat.

   I think everybody should have a turn on the computer.

2. Circle the correct spelling of the word **everybody**.
   Put an X on the words that are not correct.

   everybody   everybudy   evrybody   everybody   everyboddy   everybody

   averybody   everibody   everybody   everybody   evrybudy   everybody

   How many correct words did you find? _____

3. How many small words can you make using the letters in **everybody**?

   _____

   _____

   How many words did you make? _____

4. Fill in the blanks. Use the lifelong word where it is appropriate.

   _____ in my family gets to pick a movie on their birthday.

   What does everybody in my family get to pick on their birthday?

   _____ gets to pick a _____ on their

   _____.

   The bus driver said that _____ should sit down on the bus.

   Who said that everybody should sit down?

   The _____ driver said that _____ should sit down on the

   _____.

   The girl gave _____ in the class an invitation to the party.

   What did everybody in the class get?

   _____ in the class got an _____ to the party.

Name _____

favorite

1. Circle the word **favorite** in the sentences.

   My favorite animal is a horse.

   Pizza Barn makes my favorite pizza!

   I like to read my favorite book over and over.

2. Unscramble the word. On the line below, write the numbers in order that correspond with the correctly spelled word.

o	e	t	a	f	i	r	v
1	2	3	4	5	6	7	8

   _____

3. Write three or four complete sentences that describe your **favorite** toy. Then, draw a picture of the toy.

   _____

   _____

   _____

   _____

   _____

first

1. Circle the word **first** in the sentences.

   My sister is in the first grade.

   I like to be first in line for the water fountain.

   My mother washes the dishes first,
      then she dries them.

2. Fill in the blanks. Use the lifelong word where it is appropriate.

   The _____ time I tried to ski, I fell down a lot.

   When did I fall down a lot?

   I fell down a _____ the _____ time I tried to _____.

   We can play, but _____ I must clean my room.

   When can I play?

   We can _____, but _____ I have to clean my
   _____.

   The _____ thing I do in the morning is brush my teeth.

   What do I do first in the morning?

   In the morning, _____ I brush my teeth.

3. Write the word **first** letter by letter.

   ⓕ

Name _____

friend

1. Circle the word **friend** in the sentences.

   My best friend is Chris.

   I invited one friend to go with me to the game.

   Franco and his friend played ball in the park.

2. Write the word **friend** five times.

   _____ _____ _____

   _____ _____

3. Unscramble the word. On the line below, write the numbers in order that correspond with the correctly spelled word.

r	e	d	n	i	f
1	2	3	4	5	6

   _____

4. Write three or four complete sentences that tell about a good **friend** of yours. What do you and your **friend** like to do? What do you like about your **friend**? Draw a picture of your friend.

   _____

   _____

   _____

   _____

Name_____

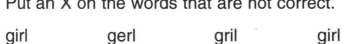

girl

1. Circle the word **girl** in the sentences.

   The girl went to the store to buy a new dress.

   My mother had a baby girl.

   When my aunt was a little girl, she liked to play ball.

2. Circle the correct spelling of the word **girl**.
   Put an X on the words that are not correct.

   girl   gerl   gril   girl   girle   girl

   gyrl   jirl   girl   gril   gril   girl

   How many correct words did you find? _____

3. Use the word **girl** in complete sentences to describe the following picture.

_____

_____

_____

_____

Name_____

goes

1. Circle the word **goes** in the sentences.

   My dad goes to work every morning.

   My sister goes really fast with her rollerblades.

   The time goes fast when we're playing.

2. Write the word **goes** five times.

   _____   _____   _____

   _____   _____

3. Circle the correct spelling of the word **goes**.
   Put an X on the words that are not correct.

   gose   goes   goees   goes   goess   goes

   goes   gos   goes   goes   goese   goes

   How many correct words did you find? _____

4. Unscramble the word. On the line below, write the numbers in order that correspond
   with the correctly spelled word.

   s   o   g   e
   1   2   3   4

   _____

5. Write the word **goes** letter by letter.

grade

1. Circle the word **grade** in the sentences.

   The fifth grade teacher at our school is Mr. Johnson.

   I hope I get a good grade on my report.

   I will be in sixth grade next year.

   5th Grade
   Mr. Johnson
   Welcome!

2. Circle the correct spelling of the word **grade**.
   Put an X on the words that are not correct.

grade	grad	grayde	grade	gade	grade
gradde	grade	grayde	grade	grade	graide

   How many correct words did you find? _____

3. How many small words can you make using the letters in **grade**?

   _____

   _____

   How many words did you make? _____

4. Fill in the blanks. Use the lifelong word where it is appropriate.

   My _____ was a B on the math test.

   What was my grade on the math test?

   My _____ was a B on the _____ test.

   My little brother is in the first _____.

   What grade is my little brother in?

   My little _____ is in the first _____.

   I got a good _____ on my report card.

   How was my report card?

   I got a good _____ on my report _____.

Name_____

guess

1. Circle the word **guess** in the sentences.

   Can you guess what I'm holding behind my back?

   I guess no one is at home today.

   It's raining, so I guess we will stay inside today.

2. Unscramble the word. On the line below, write the
   numbers in order that correspond with the
   correctly spelled word.

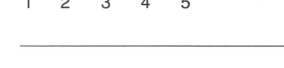

e	s	u	g	s
1	2	3	4	5

   _____

3. Find the word **guess** five times.

f	g	m	g	u	e	s	s	o	x	n
h	u	l	c	m	o	c	o	m	z	w
r	e	c	m	g	u	e	s	s	l	g
l	s	c	e	h	l	o	c	h	t	u
f	s	l	o	g	f	t	r	o	g	e
l	o	w	g	u	e	s	s	q	s	s
p	r	o	j	e	a	r	m	h	r	s

haven't

1. Circle the word **haven't** in the sentences.

   I haven't got a pencil.

   We haven't finished reading the book yet.

   Let me know if you haven't gotten the magazine you ordered.

2. Fill in the blanks. Use the lifelong word where it is appropriate.

   I _____ got enough money to buy the bike.

   Why can't I buy the bike?

   I can't buy the _____ because I _____ got enough money.

   I _____ finished my homework yet.

   What haven't I finished yet?

   I _____ finished my _____ yet.

   We wanted to make cookies, but we _____ got any sugar.

   Why can't we make cookies?

   We can't make _____ because we _____ got any sugar.

3. Write the word **haven't** letter by letter.

   _____

   _____ _____

   _____ _____ _____

   _____ _____ _____ _____

   _____ _____ _____ _____ _____

   _____ _____ _____ _____ _____ _____

   _____ _____ _____ _____ _____ _____ _____

   (h)

Name_____

having

1. Circle the word **having** in the sentences.

We were having fun in the swimming pool.

I am having trouble reaching the can on the top shelf.

Mary is having a party on Saturday.

2. Circle the correct spelling of the word **having**.
   Put an X on the words that are not correct.

| havving | haveing | having | haveing | having | having |
| having | halfving | havving | having | haveing | having |

How many correct words did you find? _____

3. Find the word **having** five times.

h	o	h	a	v	i	n	g	o	u	t
a	m	t	e	s	s	n	p	r	i	n
v	l	o	h	m	i	h	l	r	s	t
i	s	t	a	v	h	a	v	i	n	g
n	o	t	a	m	x	v	q	r	x	t
g	s	h	i	m	o	i	g	h	m	s
l	o	m	h	a	v	i	n	g	c	x

Good Apple GA 13011

hear

1. Circle the word **hear** in the sentences.

   Can you hear the birds singing?

   I did not hear what the teacher said.

   Thomas likes to hear the music on the radio.

2. Circle the correct spelling of the word **hear**.
   Put an X on the words that are not correct.

hear	haer	heer	hear	her	hear
hear	heare	hear	here	hier	hear

   How many correct words did you find? _____

3. How many small words can you make using the letters in **hear**?

   _____

   _____

   How many words did you make? _____

4. Fill in the blanks. Use the lifelong word where it is appropriate.

   If you come closer, I could _____ you better.

   How can I hear you better?

   I could _____ you better, if you come _____.

   I want you to _____ the new song on the radio.

   What do I want you to hear?

   I want you to _____ the new _____ on the radio.

   My grandfather can't _____ everything.

   Who can't hear everything?

   My _____ can't _____ everything.

Name_____

heard

1. Circle the word **heard** in the sentences.

   I have never heard that song before.
   The children heard the birds singing.
   We heard that it was going to rain today.

2. Unscramble the word. On the line below, write the numbers in order that correspond with the correctly spelled word.

r	d	a	h	e
1	2	3	4	5

   _____

3. Find the word **heard** five times.

a	l	i	m	c	g	w	s	h	r	d
f	h	e	a	r	d	l	m	e	w	k
a	h	l	i	e	n	s	o	a	h	b
s	e	f	h	e	a	r	d	r	c	x
l	a	d	m	i	h	l	c	d	o	h
f	r	o	h	e	a	r	d	o	f	c
s	d	m	l	i	m	c	q	q	s	i

Name_____

here

1. Circle the word **here** in the sentences.

    Come here, Rover!
    The circus will be coming here soon.
    Here is the book you wanted.

2. Write the word **here** five times.

    _____   _____   _____

    _____   _____

3. Fill in the blanks. Use the lifelong word where it is appropriate.

    My uncle is coming over _____ tonight.

    When is my uncle coming?

    My _____ is coming over _____ tonight.

    _____ is the newspaper.

    Where is the newspaper?

    The _____ is _____.

    I will put your pencil right _____ on the desk.

    Where will I put your pencil?

    I will put your _____ right _____ on the desk.

4. Write the word **here** letter by letter.

Name_____

1. Circle the word **hour** in the sentences.

   My father will be here in one hour.

   This television show lasts one hour.

   I have only one hour to get my work done.

2. Write the word **hour** five times.

   _____   _____   _____

   _____   _____

3. Unscramble the word. On the line below, write the numbers in order that correspond with the correctly spelled word.

u	r	h	o
1	2	3	4

   _____

4. Find the word **hour** five times.

f	m	a	l	h	o	u	r	x	r	w
c	r	o	m	w	c	m	l	u	g	d
x	t	h	o	u	r	m	o	j	f	l
l	i	h	c	t	h	h	i	f	w	a
f	c	o	l	h	o	u	r	s	m	b
t	m	u	c	o	s	l	b	d	q	a
d	a	r	t	u	f	a	n	p	g	y

house

1. Circle the word **house** in the sentences.

   We live in a yellow house.

   Don't let the dog get in the house.

   That house has a broken window.

2. Circle the correct spelling of the word **house**.
   Put an X on the words that are not correct.

howse	housse	house	houze	huose	house
house	hows	houze	house	house	houze

   How many correct words did you find? _____

3. Write three or four complete sentences that describe the perfect **house**. What would it look like? Where would it be? Draw a picture of your perfect house.

   _____

   _____

   _____

   _____

48

Name_____

1. Circle the word **knew** in the sentences.

   Brad knew the answer to the math problem.

   Mario knew how to put the wheel on the bike.

   I knew I was getting a puppy for my birthday.

2. Circle the correct spelling of the word **knew**.
   Put an X on the words that are not correct.

   knew   know   new   knew   knoo   knew

   knewe   knew   knew   newe   knw   knew

   How many correct words did you find? _____

3. How many small words can you make using the letters in **knew**?

   _____

   _____

   How many words did you make? _____

4. Fill in the blanks. Use the lifelong word where it is appropriate.

   I wish I _____ the answer to the problem.

   What do I wish I knew?

   I wish I _____ the answer to the _____.

   The teacher _____ that the class was having a party for her.

   What did the teacher know?

   The teacher _____ that the class was having a _____ _____ for her.

   Mrs. Martinez _____ that it was going to rain, so she took an umbrella
   to work.

   Why did Mrs. Martinez take an umbrella to work?

   She took an _____ to work because she _____ it was
   going to rain.

know

1. Circle the word **know** in the sentences.

   I know how to build a birdhouse.

   Do you know my friend, Pat?

   Lyn doesn't know how to use a computer.

2. Unscramble the word. On the line below, write the numbers in order that correspond with the correctly spelled word.

   w   o   k   n
   1   2   3   4

   _____

3. Find the word **know** five times.

f	m	b	d	m	i	l	h	r	c	r
f	k	m	k	n	o	w	l	b	d	f
b	n	l	i	m	c	b	h	q	s	s
f	o	l	w	k	n	o	w	k	h	d
r	w	o	k	s	t	u	v	n	b	x
d	n	r	n	l	m	i	q	o	b	u
k	r	t	o	f	q	w	e	w	t	l

Name _____

1. Circle the word **language** in the sentences.

   Arthur's mother speaks a different language.
   You should always use good language.
   I can read a few words in another language.

2. Write the word **language** five times.

   _____   _____   _____

   _____   _____

3. How many small words can you make using the letters in **language**?

   _____

   _____

   How many words did you make? _____

4. Fill in the blanks. Use the lifelong word where it is appropriate.

   We are studying the English _____ in school.

   What are we studying in school?

   We are _____ the English _____ in school.

   I can read this story in another _____.

   What can I read in another language?

   I can read this _____ in another _____.

   You should make sure that you use good _____ all the time.

   What should you use all the time?

   You should always use good _____.

Name_____

many

1. Circle the word **many** in the sentences.

   My sister has many friends.
   I have too many books to carry.
   There are many flowers in the garden.

2. Write the word **many** five times.

   _____   _____   _____

   _____   _____

3. Circle the correct spelling of the word **many**.
   Put an X on the words that are not correct.

   many   manny   many   meny   many   mony

   manny   many   menne   manny   many   many

   How many correct words did you find? _____

4. Unscramble the word. On the line below, write the numbers in order that
   correspond with the correctly spelled word.

   y   a   m   n
   1   2   3   4

   _____

5. Write the word **many** letter by letter.

name

1. Circle the word **name** in the sentences.

   My name is Sara.

   What did you name your new puppy?

   Write your name on the top of your paper.

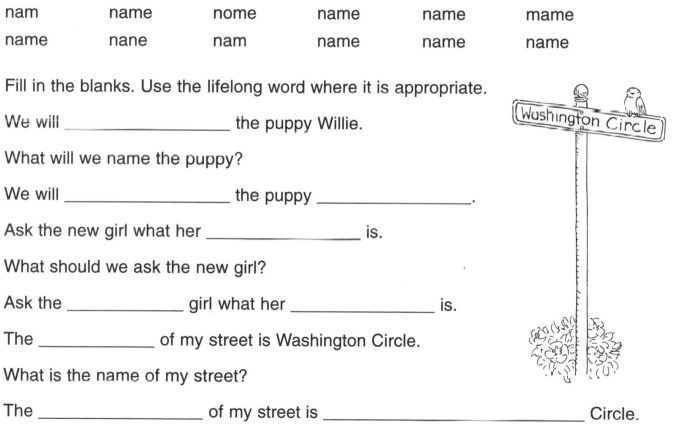

2. Circle the correct spelling of the word **name**.
   Put an X on the words that are not correct.

nam	name	nome	name	name	mame
name	nane	nam	name	name	name

3. Fill in the blanks. Use the lifelong word where it is appropriate.

   We will _____ the puppy Willie.

   What will we name the puppy?

   We will _____ the puppy _____.

   Ask the new girl what her _____ is.

   What should we ask the new girl?

   Ask the _____ girl what her _____ is.

   The _____ of my street is Washington Circle.

   What is the name of my street?

   The _____ of my street is _____ Circle.

new

1. Circle the word **new** in the sentences.

   My dad got a new car.

   Do you like my new haircut?

   We went to the store for new shoes.

2. Unscramble the word. On the line below, write the numbers in order that correspond with the correctly spelled word.

w	n	e
1	2	3

   _____

3. Write three or four sentences that tell what **new** things you would buy if you suddenly got $1,000 for a gift. Where would you go shopping? Draw a picture of one of the things you would buy.

   _____

   _____

   _____

   _____

none

1. Circle the word **none** in the sentences.

   None of us wants to do extra homework.

   My mother asked who wanted to do the dishes, but none of us did.

   Tanya looked in the cabinet for some cans of soup, but there were none there.

2. Unscramble the word. On the line below, write the numbers in order that correspond with the correctly spelled word.

n	n	o	e
1	2	3	4

   _____

3. Find the word **none** five times.

f	n	o	n	e	t	r	q	w	e	r
l	k	n	m	c	i	l	t	y	u	i
f	t	o	m	h	m	n	u	i	o	p
t	r	n	d	r	l	o	a	s	d	f
k	s	e	f	l	m	n	g	h	j	k
w	e	n	o	n	e	e	z	x	c	v
b	n	o	n	e	t	l	b	n	m	k

often

1. Circle the word **often** in the sentences.

   We go to the movies very often.
   Our class often gets to go on a field trip.
   It often rains in the spring.

2. Write the word **often** five times.

   _____ _____ _____

   _____ _____

3. Fill in the blanks. Use the lifelong word where it is appropriate.

   Our family goes to the library fairly _____.

   Where do we often go?

   Our _____ goes to the library _____.

   My state _____ has a lot of snow in the winter.

   When do we have a lot of snow?

   My state _____ has a lot of snow in the _____.

   I hope that you will come to my house _____ for a visit.

   What do I hope that you will do?

   I hope that _____ will visit my house _____.

4. Write the word **often** letter by letter.

   ___ ___

   ___ ___ ___

   ___ ___ ___ ___

   ___ ___ ___ ___ ___

   ___ ___ ___ ___ ___ ___

Name_____

······· **once** ·······

1. Circle the word **once** in the sentences.

   Once upon a time, there was a princess and a frog.
   My friend rode on an elephant once at the zoo.
   I have only been to the park once.

2. Write the word **once** five times.

   _____   _____   _____

   _____   _____

3. Circle the correct spelling of the word **once**.
   Put an X on the words that are not correct.

   unce   once   onse   once   onese   once
   once   onece   wonce   once   unce   once

   How many correct words did you find? _____

4. Unscramble the word. On the line below, write the numbers in order that correspond
   with the correctly spelled word.

   e   n   o   c
   1   2   3   4

   _____

5. Write the word **once** letter by letter.

Name _____

only

1. Circle the word **only** in the sentences.

   I have only one brother.

   It will only be a minute before we leave.

   If I only had a dollar, I could buy that toy.

2. Circle the correct spelling of the word **only**.
   Put an X on the words that are not correct.

onlly	only	ownly	only	onlie	only
only	anly	ownle	only	onlee	only

   How many correct words did you find? _____

3. How many small words can you make using the letters in **only**?

   _____

   _____

   How many words did you make? _____

4. Fill in the blanks. Use the lifelong word where it is appropriate.

   We could go on that ride if we
   _____ had a ticket.

   What could we do with a ticket?

   If we _____ had a ticket,
   we could go on that _____.

   Haruka has _____ one grandfather.

   How many grandfathers does Haruka have?

   Haruka has _____ one _____.

   I _____ have to do one page of math homework.

   How much math homework do I have to do?

   I _____ have to do _____ page of math homework.

Name _____

1. Circle the word **our** in the sentences.

   We live in a big house because our family is large.

   Our dog ate the flowers in the garden.

   My mother always says that our car is too dirty.

2. Unscramble the word. On the line below, write the numbers in order that correspond with the correctly spelled word.

   r   o   u
   1   2   3

   _____

3. Find the word **our** five times.

k	m	l	o	x	h	m	f	s	o	j
f	t	h	u	m	s	o	v	g	d	o
o	u	r	r	h	t	u	p	f	o	j
m	a	n	o	u	r	r	b	x	i	h
k	o	u	r	p	s	y	b	c	o	k
g	a	r	k	i	m	t	l	k	j	h
s	a	e	f	i	h	b	c	g	k	d

Name _____

people

1. Circle the word **people** in the sentences.

   There were many people on the bus.
   My dog does not like people he doesn't know.
   Most people like to eat pizza.

2. Write the word **people** five times.

   _____   _____   _____

   _____   _____

3. Use the word **people** in complete sentences to describe the following picture.

   _____

   _____

   _____

   _____

Name_____

1. Circle the word **picture** in the sentences.

   Please hang the picture on the wall.
   My aunt will take a picture of us.
   Do you like this picture that I drew?

2. Write the word **picture** five times.

   _____   _____   _____

   _____   _____

3. Circle the correct spelling of the word **picture**.
   Put an X on the words that are not correct.

   picture   pictre   pictore   picture   pickture   picture
   picture   picksure   picture   picture   picture   picure

   How many correct words did you find? _____

4. Draw a **picture** that shows something you really enjoy doing.

Name_____

pretty

1. Circle the word **pretty** in the sentences.

   My mother is a pretty woman.
   This is a pretty picture.
   What a pretty day it is today!

2. Circle the correct spelling of the word **pretty**.
   Put an X on the words that are not correct.

   pritty   prety   pretty   pretty   prety   pretty

   prettie   pretty   pretty   pritty   pretty   pretty

   How many correct words did you find? _____

3. Fill in the blanks. Use the lifelong word where it is appropriate.

   Mei bought a _____ picture.

   What did Mei buy?

   Mei _____ a _____ picture.

   The snow on the trees is very _____.

   What makes the trees pretty?

   The _____ on the trees is very _____.

   David thinks Mookie is a very _____ cat.

   What does David think about Mookie?

   He thinks _____ is a very _____ cat.

4. Write three or four complete sentences that describe someone who you think is pretty.

   _____

   _____

   _____

   _____

Name _____

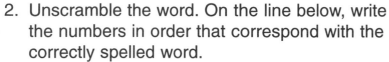
1. Circle the word **probably** in the sentences.

   My father will probably be home around 5 o'clock.

   I can probably finish my homework in a half hour.

   It will probably rain today, so I will take my umbrella.

2. Unscramble the word. On the line below, write the numbers in order that correspond with the correctly spelled word.

p	l	y	b	b	a	r	o
1	2	3	4	5	6	7	8

_____

3. Find the word **probably** five times.

f	p	r	o	b	a	b	l	y	i	p
a	h	m	p	r	o	b	a	b	l	y
p	m	h	k	i	s	l	i	h	m	o
r	s	p	r	o	b	a	b	l	y	b
o	d	s	h	p	c	h	a	r	t	a
b	p	r	o	b	a	b	l	y	a	b
a	g	e	p	r	o	b	a	b	l	y

Name_____

receive

1. Circle the word **receive** in the sentences.

   I hope I receive a letter from my friend today.

   My sister wants to receive a phone call from her boyfriend.

   Did you receive the package I sent you?

2. Fill in the blanks. Use the lifelong word where it is appropriate.

   Karen hopes to _____ a beautiful ring for her birthday.

   What does Karen hope for?

   She hopes to _____ a ring for her _____.

   I did not _____ any mail today.

   What didn't I receive today

   I didn't _____ any mail _____.

   Throw me the ball, and I'll try to _____ it.

   What will I hope to receive?

   If you _____ me the ball, I'll try to _____ it.

3. Write the word **receive** letter by letter.

   ⓡ

Name _____

remember

1. Circle the word **remember** in the sentences.

   I remember when I was at camp last summer.

   Do you remember the name of the new boy?

   I hope my mother will remember to pick up some ice cream from the store.

2. Write the word **remember** five times.

   _____   _____   _____

   _____   _____

3. How many small words can you make using the letters in remember?

   _____

   _____

   How many words did you make? _____

4. Circle the correct spelling of the word **remember**.
   Put an X on the words that are not correct.

   remember   ramember   rimember   remember   remember   remmember

   rember   remember   remember   remomber   remember   remembur

   How many correct words did you find? _____

5. Draw a picture of something special you remember. Write one or two complete sentences about it.

   _____

   _____

   _____

   _____

Name _____

right

1. Circle the word **right** in the sentences.

   Raise your right hand if you need a pencil.
   Turn right at the corner to get to my house.
   I know that this is the right answer.

2. Circle the correct spelling of the word **right**.
   Put an X on the words that are not correct.

righ	right	rite	right	right	rihgtt
right	right	rige	righte	right	right

   How many correct words did you find? _____

3. How many small words can you make using the letters in **right**?

   _____

   _____

   How many words did you make? _____

4. Fill in the blanks. Use the lifelong word where it is appropriate.

   I know the _____ answer to the math problem.

   What do I know the answer to?

   I know the _____ answer to the _____ problem.

   It is important to know _____ from wrong.

   What is important to know?

   It is _____ to know _____ from wrong.

   Be sure to take the _____ trail so you don't get lost.

   What should you do?

   Take the _____ trail so you don't get _____.

said

1. Circle the word **said** in the sentences.

   My teacher said that we could go outside for recess.

   I could not hear what the man on the radio said.

   Bob said, "Everyone can have more pizza!"

2. Unscramble the word. On the line below, write the numbers in order that correspond with the correctly spelled word.

d	s	i	a
1	2	3	4

   _____

3. Find the word **said** five times.

s	a	i	d	f	s	a	i	d	s	l
l	i	m	d	l	e	m	a	n	d	x
w	o	s	m	i	h	l	i	i	h	v
f	q	a	j	i	o	d	a	r	c	o
l	t	i	d	i	c	s	z	a	s	o
r	t	d	s	a	i	d	o	l	c	o
p	q	i	o	n	l	d	a	n	r	w

school

1. Circle the word **school** in the sentences.

   I like to go to school.

   There is a student in our school who is from France.

   The basketball game is in the school gym tonight.

2. Write the word **school** five times.

   _____   _____   _____

   _____   _____

3. Write the word **school** letter by letter.

   ___

   ___ ___

   ___ ___ ___

   ___ ___ ___ ___

   ___ ___ ___ ___ ___

   S ___ ___ ___ ___ ___ ___

4. Write one or two complete sentences that describe your **school.** What do you like about it? What do you wish were different? Draw a picture of your school.

   _____

   _____

   _____

   _____

should

1. Circle the word **should** in the sentences.

   You should wash your hands before you eat.
   Do you think we should wash the car?
   I think we should dive off the diving board.

2. Fill in the blanks. Use the lifelong word where it is appropriate.

   The teacher said we _____ put our names on our papers.

   What should we put our names on?

   The teacher said that we _____ put our _____ on our papers.

   A friend _____ keep a promise.

   What should a friend do?

   A friend _____ keep a _____.

   My parents think we _____ do our homework right away.

   When should we do our homework?

   My parents think we _____ do our homework _____ away.

3. Write the word **should** letter by letter.

   S

Name_____

1. Circle the word **some** in the sentences.

   Would you like some of my pizza?
   If you have some time, let's play basketball.
   My sister had some friends over for a party.

2. Write the word **some** five times.

   _____   _____   _____

   _____   _____

3. Circle the correct spelling of the word **some**.
   Put an X on the words that are not correct.

some	some	sume	sum	some	some
some	some	come	some	summe	some

   How many correct words did you find? _____

4. Unscramble the word. On the line below, write the numbers in order that correspond
   with the correctly spelled word.

   ```
   m   s   o   e
   1   2   3   4
   ```

   _____

5. Write the word **some** letter by letter.

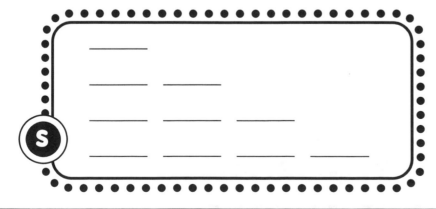

Name _____

something

1. Circle the word **something** in the sentences.

   There is something for you in this box.
   Tell me something about your favorite movie.
   Something is making a big noise upstairs!

2. Circle the correct spelling of the word **something**.
   Put an X on the words that are not correct.

   somthing   something   sumthing   soemthing   something   someting

   something   someting   something   sumething   something   sumtheng

   How many correct words did you find? _____

3. How many small words can you make using the letters in **something**?

   _____

   _____

   How many words did you make? _____

4. Fill in the blanks. Use the lifelong word where it is appropriate.

   I want _____ chocolate for dessert.

   What do I want for dessert?

   I want _____ chocolate for _____.

   Jenny bought _____ for her mother's birthday.

   Why did Jenny buy something for her mother?

   Jenny bought _____ for her mother's _____.

   Fred heard _____ making a noise in the yard.

   Where did Fred hear a noise?

   Fred heard _____ making a noise in the _____.

store

1. Circle the word **store** in the sentences.

   My brother went to the store to buy some apples.

   The store had a big sale on jeans.

   We got some potato chips at the store.

2. Unscramble the word. On the line below, write the numbers in order that correspond with the correctly spelled word.

   t   e   r   o   s
   1   2   3   4   5

   _____

3. Write three or four complete sentences that tell what you would buy if you had $1,000 to spend at your favorite **store.** Draw a picture of yourself shopping in the store with the $1,000.

   _____

   _____

   _____

   _____

Name_____

1. Circle the word **suppose** in the sentences.

   I suppose I should get out of bed since it's noon.

   How do you suppose the criminal stole the money from the bank?

   Suppose you were invisible for a day. What would you do?

2. Circle the correct spelling of the word **suppose**.
   Put an X on the words that are not correct.

supose	suppoze	suppose	suppose	seppose	suppose
suppose	suppize	suppose	supose	suppose	supppose

   How many correct words did you find? _____

3. How many small words can you make using the letters in **suppose**?

   _____

   _____

   How many words did you make? _____

4. Fill in the blanks. Use the lifelong word where it is appropriate.

   I _____ I should wash the dishes.

   What should I do?

   I _____ I should _____ the dishes.

   _____ you could fly. Wouldn't that be fun?

   What would be fun?

   _____ you could fly. That would be _____!

   I _____ my parents will be home soon.

   Who will be home soon?

   I _____ my _____ will be home soon.

Name_____

surprise

1. Circle the word **surprise** in the sentences.

   Let's give Ben a surprise party!

   I will surprise my teacher with some flowers.

   My dad likes to surprise my mom by cleaning up the house.

2. Unscramble the word. On the line below, write the numbers in order that correspond with the correctly spelled word.

e	s	i	p	r	u	s	r
1	2	3	4	5	6	7	8

   _____

3. Use the word **surprise** in complete sentences to describe the following picture.

   _____

   _____

   _____

   _____

Name _____

1. Circle the word **taught** in the sentences.

My father taught art at our high school.

My brother taught me how to play football.

Frank taught everyone in the class how to draw a horse.

2. Write the word **taught** five times.

_____   _____   _____

_____   _____

3. Unscramble the word. On the line below, write the numbers in order that correspond with the correctly spelled word.

a	g	h	t	t	u
1	2	3	4	5	6

_____

4. Find the word **taught** five times.

d	o	t	m	c	l	o	l	e	h	a
l	r	a	c	h	c	m	e	g	t	f
l	o	u	g	c	l	x	h	r	a	s
c	i	g	t	a	u	g	h	t	u	i
m	o	h	t	c	m	e	w	l	g	f
c	n	t	a	u	g	h	t	h	h	v
c	t	a	u	g	h	t	l	o	t	s

teacher

1. Circle the word **teacher** in the sentences.

   My teacher is a tall man.

   I will ask the teacher for some help.

   We played basketball outside with my teacher.

2. Write the word **teacher** letter by letter.

3. Write one of two complete sentences that tell about your favorite **teacher.** Why do you like him or her? What does he or she teach? Draw a picture of your special teacher.

   _____

   _____

   _____

   _____

   _____

   _____

   _____

76

Name_____

1. Circle the word **their** in the sentences.

   Our neighbors paid us to wash their car.
   Our other neighbors paid us to walk their dog.
   The teacher told everyone to put their books away.

2. Fill in the blanks. Use the lifelong word where it is appropriate.

   My parents want us to clean _____ car.

   What do our parents want us to do?

   My _____ want us to clean _____ car.

   The football team had _____ practice at 5:00.

   When did the team practice?

   The football team had _____ practice at _____.

   My sisters want to have _____ own phone in _____room.

   What do my sisters want?

   My _____ want to have _____ own phone in _____ room.

3. Write the word **their** letter by letter.

   _____

   _____ _____

   _____ _____ _____

   _____ _____ _____ _____

   _____ _____ _____ _____ _____

Name_____

there

1. Circle the word **there** in the sentences.

   Sit over there by the tree.

   There are five people in the car.

   Do you know if there are any crayons in the box?

2. Write the word **there** five times.

   _____ _____ _____

   _____ _____

3. Circle the correct spelling of the word **there.**
   Put an X on the words that are not correct.

ther	there	theire	there	theer	there
there	tere	there	theer	there	their

   How many correct words did you find? _____

4. Find the word **there** five times.

f	i	c	l	t	w	o	h	c	m	e	b
t	h	e	r	e	c	i	m	l	r	q	t
w	c	i	e	b	s	c	r	e	t	o	h
f	h	t	h	e	r	e	h	a	m	n	e
c	t	c	i	m	l	t	h	c	o	v	r
c	h	e	h	t	h	e	r	e	c	x	e
w	e	f	r	h	o	k	l	c	a	l	t

Name _____

1. Circle the word **they're** in the sentences.

   My parents said that they're going to a movie tonight.
   I think that they're going for a walk.
   The dogs act as though they're hungry.

2. Circle the correct spelling of the word **they're.**
   Put an X on the words that are not correct.

they're	theyr	thay're	they're	they'are	they're
they're	they're	thay'r	they'r	they're	they're

   How many correct words did you find? _____

3. How many small words can you make using the letters in **they're**?

   _____

   _____

   _____

   How many words did you make? _____

4. Fill in the blanks. Use the lifelong word where it is appropriate.

   Someone didn't feed the fish and now _____ dead.

   What happened to the fish?

   Someone didn't _____ the fish and now _____ dead.

   My friends said that _____ going bowling.

   Who is going bowling?

   My _____ said _____ going bowling.

   I like boys, but only when _____ polite.

   When do I like boys?

   I like _____ only when _____ polite.

thought

1. Circle the word **thought** in the sentences.

   Sandy thought today was Saturday, so she slept in.

   I thought about my grandmother today.

   Tony thought of a new way to draw using the computer.

2. Unscramble the word. On the line below, write the numbers in order that correspond with the correctly spelled word.

t	t	o	u	h	h	g
1	2	3	4	5	6	7

   _____

3. Find the word **thought** five times.

f	l	t	t	h	o	u	g	h	t	z
c	a	h	c	k	i	m	l	t	r	m
c	t	o	c	t	h	g	u	o	h	t
e	i	u	c	h	o	u	c	b	c	n
o	t	g	t	h	o	u	g	h	t	r
c	i	h	c	h	x	r	l	i	h	x
c	o	t	h	o	u	g	h	t	o	w

80

threw

1. Circle the word **threw** in the sentences.

   The baseball player threw the ball to the catcher.
   The little girl threw her doll on the floor.
   I threw the ball back to my partner.

2. Circle the correct spelling of the word **threw.**
   Put an X on the words that are not correct.

threw	throw	threwe	threw	threw	throo
threw	thew	threq	throo	threw	thew

   How many correct words did you find? _____

3. How many small words can you make using the letters in **threw**?

   _____

   _____

   How many words did you make? _____

4. Use the word **threw** in complete sentences to describe the following picture.

Name_____

through

1. Circle the word **through** in the sentences.

   I am almost through reading the book.
   The ball went through the window and broke it.
   At the circus, the lion jumped through the hoop.

2. Write the word **through** five times.

   _____ _____ _____

   _____ _____

3. Unscramble the word. On the line below, write the numbers in order that correspond with the correctly spelled word.

t	h	h	o	u	r	g
1	2	3	4	5	6	7

   _____

4. Write the word **through** letter by letter.

Name_____

· **to** · · · · · · · · · · · · · · · · ·

1. Circle the word **to** in the sentences.

   George and I are going to the store.
   I have to clean my room after school.
   Amy forgot to brush her teeth.

2. Fill in the blanks. Use the lifelong word where it is appropriate.

   Brian wants _____ go on vacation to Hawaii.

   Where would Brian like to go?

   Brian would like _____ go on a _____ to Hawaii.

   Lucy and Tanesha went _____ the park to run.

   Where did the girls go to run?

   Lucy and Tanesha went _____ the _____ to run.

   Don't forget _____ bring a pencil to class.

   What shouldn't you forget to bring?

   Don't forget _____ bring a _____ to class.

3. Find the word **to** five times.

t	o	f	m	c	h	l	r	i	v	h
m	l	t	m	i	c	s	t	r	d	j
f	o	o	c	i	g	b	c	w	g	d
f	w	i	c	x	z	l	k	b	y	f
s	t	t	o	i	u	y	c	v	r	s
f	o	c	t	t	o	h	x	m	b	h
l	h	c	y	f	s	p	j	r	v	m

together

1. Circle the word **together** in the sentences.

   We can work together on our book reports.

   My best friend thinks it is fun to go to the movies together.

   I like to mix ice cream and cookies together.

2. Circle the correct spelling of the word **together.**
   Put an X on the words that are not correct.

together	togeher	tagether	toogether	together	together
together	togather	together	together	togezther	togetther

   How many correct words did you find? _____

3. How many small words can you make using the letters in **together**?

   _____

   _____

   How many words did you make? _____

4. Fill in the blanks. Use the lifelong word where it is appropriate.

   We can ride on this bike _____.

   What can we ride on?

   We can _____ on this bike _____.

   Our family sat _____ at the concert last week.

   Who sat together?

   Our _____ sat _____ at the concert last week.

   It's fun to play basketball _____.

   What is fun to play together?

   It's fun to _____ basketball _____.

Name_____

tomorrow

1. Circle the word **tomorrow** in the sentences.

I am so glad that tomorrow is Saturday.

This homework is due tomorrow.

My mother said this room better be clean by tomorrow.

2. How many small words can you make using the letters in **tomorrow**?

_____

_____

How many words did you make? _____

3. Find the word **tomorrow** five times.

f	t	o	m	o	r	r	o	w	s	h
d	h	t	o	m	o	r	r	o	w	w
e	d	t	c	l	o	d	a	r	o	p
e	l	w	o	r	r	o	m	o	t	r
t	o	m	o	r	r	o	w	b	o	b
m	a	o	s	c	r	l	b	z	r	d
t	w	w	o	r	r	o	m	o	t	a

Name _____

tonight

1. Circle the word **tonight** in the sentences.

   We are going to the movies tonight.

   My aunt and uncle are coming to visit tonight.

   Barbara has to babysit tonight for her sister.

2. Write the word **tonight** five times.

   _____ _____ _____

   _____ _____

3. Unscramble the word. On the line below, write the numbers in order that correspond
   with the correctly spelled word.

i	t	g	o	n	t	h
1	2	3	4	5	6	7

   _____

4. Write the word **tonight** letter by letter.

Name _____

1. Circle the word **too** in the sentences.

   My little brother wants to go too.

   I have too many books to carry.

   It is too wet outside for us to play.

2. Write the word **too** five times.

   _____   _____   _____

   _____   _____

3. Circle the correct spelling of the word **too.**
   Put an X on the words that are not correct.

   too   oto   toe   tuu   too   tu

   to   too   tou   tu   too   tooo

   How many correct words did you find? _____

4. Fill in the blanks. Use the lifelong word where it is appropriate.

   George was _____ sick to go to the football game.

   Why didn't George go to the football game?

   George was _____ sick to go to the _____ game.

   My little brother wanted to go to the movies _____.

   What did my little brother want to do?

   My little _____ wanted _____ go to the movies _____.

   Andre ate his sandwich, then he ate mine _____.

   What did Andre eat?

   Andre ate his _____ then he ate mine _____.

Name_____

1. Circle the word **two** in the sentences.

   I have two eyes, two ears, and two legs.

   There are two squirrels playing in the yard.

   In two days, we are going on vacation.

2. Circle the correct spelling of the word **two.**
   Put an X on the words that are not correct.

tow	two	too	towe	two	twoo
two	tow	twow	two	two	towe

   How many correct words did you find? _____

3. Fill in the blanks. Use the lifelong word where it is appropriate.

   Karla needs to bring _____ pencils to class.

   What should Karla bring to class?

   Karla needs to bring _____ pencils to _____.

   It will be my birthday in only _____ days.

   When is my birthday?

   My _____ is in only _____ days.

   For_____ dollars, I can buy this book.

   What can I buy for two dollars?

   I can buy this _____ for _____ dollars.

Name_____

1. Circle the word **until** in the sentences.

   We can't go outside until our homework is done.

   The dog must stay outside until he is housebroken.

   There are only two weeks until my birthday.

2. Circle the correct spelling of the word **until.**
   Put an X on the words that are not correct.

   unntil   until   untill   until   until   untiel

   until   untill   ontil   untel   until   until

   How many correct words did you find? _____

3. How many small words can you make using the letters in **until**?

   _____

   _____

   How many words did you make? _____

4. Fill in the blanks. Use the lifelong word where it is appropriate.

   My mother will wait for us _____ it is 5:00.

   How long will my mother wait?

   My _____ will wait for us _____ it is 5:00.

   I have to stay after school _____ my project is done.

   Why do I have to stay after school?

   I have to stay after school _____ my _____ is done.

   George can't go to college _____ he finishes high school.

   When can George go to college?

   George can't go to college _____ he finishes _____.

Name_____

1. Circle the word **used** in the sentences.

   This is a used car.

   My brother used my bike and now it is broken.

   Someone used my reading book yesterday.

2. Write the word **used** five times.

   _____   _____   _____

   _____   _____

3. Unscramble the word. On the line below, write the numbers in order that correspond with the correctly spelled word.

   d   e   s   u
   1   2   3   4

   _____

4. Find the word **used** five times.

f	c	u	s	e	d	r	t	d	f	g
l	u	l	c	k	i	u	y	g	h	j
l	s	c	e	g	z	s	a	w	e	y
f	e	c	i	r	h	e	u	g	d	k
k	d	s	c	l	i	d	j	g	y	e
u	s	e	d	c	m	l	v	h	e	q
w	s	o	u	s	e	d	q	a	k	g

Name _____

very

1. Circle the word **very** in the sentences.

It was very cold outside, so we wore our winter coats.

We had a very good time at the party.

Alison is a very good artist.

2. Write the word **very** five times.

_____ _____ _____

_____ _____

3. Fill in the blanks. Use the lifelong word where it is appropriate.

We were _____ tired because we stayed up so late.

Why were we so tired?

We were _____ tired because we stayed up so _____.

If you are _____ quiet, you can get close to the birds.

What can you do if you are very quiet?

If you are _____ quiet, you can get close to the _____.

The basketball player was _____ tall.

Who was very tall?

The _____ player was _____ tall.

4. Write the word **very** letter by letter.

V

____

____ ____

____ ____ ____

____ ____ ____ ____

way

1. Circle the word **way** in the sentences.

   This is the way to my house.

   This toy is way too expensive to buy.

   I like the way you decorated your lunchbox.

2. Circle the correct spelling of the word **way.**
   Put an X on the words that are not correct.

way	waye	weiy	way	way	waay
waye	way	way	waie	waay	way

   How many correct words did you find? _____

3. Fill in the blanks. Use the lifelong word where it is appropriate.

   I like the _____ you draw those cartoons.

   What do I like the way you draw?

   I like the _____ you draw those _____.

   Be sure to turn the right _____ on the highway.

   What should you be sure to do?

   Be sure to turn the right _____ on the _____.

   Tuan likes the _____ he got his hair cut.

   What did Tuan like?

   Tuan liked the _____ he got his _____ cut.

Name_____

1. Circle the word **wear** in the sentences.

   Be sure to wear a coat outside.

   I wear the same shoes everyday.

   It is fun to wear new clothes.

2. Circle the correct spelling of the word **wear.**
   Put an X on the words that are not correct.

wear	waer	were	wear	where	wear
weare	wear	waer	wear	whear	ware

   How many correct words did you find? _____

3. Write the word **wear** letter by letter.

   (W) _____   _____   _____
        _____   _____   _____   _____
        _____   _____   _____   _____   _____

4. Write one or two complete sentences to describe what you would **wear** to a costume party. Draw a picture of your costume.

   _____

   _____

   _____

   _____

   _____

Name _____

weigh

1. Circle the word **weigh** in the sentences.

    I think my dog weighs too much.

    My mother wants to weigh the bananas before she buys them.

    How much do you think this box might weigh?

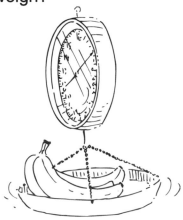

2. Unscramble the word. On the line below, write the numbers in order that correspond with the correctly spelled word.

w	h	g	e	i
1	2	3	4	5

    _____

3. Find the word **weigh** five times.

f	w	e	i	g	h	t	o	l	b	d
c	i	m	w	l	o	c	h	h	m	w
w	c	e	e	c	o	l	g	o	l	e
e	c	i	i	z	e	i	l	w	w	i
k	n	e	g	r	e	w	f	h	v	g
o	c	t	h	w	h	e	l	o	t	h
w	e	i	g	h	o	i	z	t	x	z

Name_____

1. Circle the word **we're** in the sentences.

   We're going to Canada this summer.
   I sure hope we're going outside for recess.
   The teacher said we're going home early today.

2. Fill in the blanks. Use the lifelong word where it is appropriate.

   _____ moving into a new house.

   Where are we moving?

   _____ moving into a new _____.

   My father says _____ lucky to live in America.

   What does my dad say?

   My dad says that _____ lucky to live in _____.

   _____ going to the museum on Friday.

   When are we going to the museum?

   _____ going to the _____ on Friday.

3. Write the word **we're** letter by letter.

W

95

Name_____

1. Circle the word **were** in the sentences.

   Yesterday, we were at the beach for four hours.
   The puppies were able to get out of their box.
   None of the cars were what we were looking for.

2. Write the word **were** five times.

   _____   _____   _____

        _____   _____

3. Circle the correct spelling of the word **were.**
   Put an X on the words that are not correct.

   wer   were   were   wore   werre   were

   were   were   werer   we'r   wer   werr

   How many correct words did you find? _____

4. Find the word **were** five times.

w	e	r	e	f	o	c	q	r	s	d
t	h	o	c	m	w	o	f	f	k	h
e	c	w	e	r	e	l	t	z	e	x
e	c	h	r	o	r	c	t	r	f	h
t	h	c	l	e	e	a	e	w	s	g
f	x	b	g	w	f	w	r	e	l	h
w	e	r	e	l	t	c	o	r	c	f

Name_____

1. Circle the word **when** in the sentences.

   My mother will tell us when it is time to come in.

   I don't remember when we moved to Michigan.

   When it starts to rain, be sure to get your umbrella.

2. Write the word **when** five times.

   _____   _____   _____

   _____   _____

3. Circle the correct spelling of the word **when.**
   Put an X on the words that are not correct.

   when   when   whin   whene   when   whenn

   when   wenn   when   whin   when   wen

   How many correct words did you find? _____

4. Fill in the blanks. Use the lifelong word where it is appropriate.

   We will start to run _____ the flag is waved.

   When will we start to run?

   We will start to run _____ the
   _____ is waved.

   I have to feed the dogs _____ they are hungry.

   When should I feed the dogs?

   I have to feed the dogs _____ they are _____.

   Put sunscreen on _____ it is sunny.

   When should you put sunscreen on?

   _____ it is _____, put sunscreen on.

Name_____

where

1. Circle the word **where** in the sentences.

   I will show you where we traveled using this map.

   Tim didn't know where he left his socks.

   Huma knew it was time to go.

2. Unscramble the word. On the line below, write the numbers in order that correspond with the correctly spelled word.

e	r	e	w	h
1	2	3	4	5

   _____

3. Find the word **where** five times.

f	w	h	e	r	e	l	o	m	c	t
d	a	l	c	e	w	c	h	w	t	f
d	c	h	r	w	h	c	o	h	o	j
d	c	e	c	e	e	d	f	e	c	d
c	h	l	t	o	r	f	x	r	x	v
w	h	l	c	h	e	o	c	e	s	k
f	o	x	w	h	e	r	e	o	l	n

Name _____

1. Circle the word **which** in the sentences.

   Tell me which puppy you want to take home.
   Do you remember which computer is not working right?
   I can't tell which painting is mine.

2. Fill in the blanks. Use the lifelong word where it is appropriate.

   Eli told us _____ games were the best ones.

   Who told us which games were best?

   Eli told us _____ games were the _____ ones.

   Tell me _____ hat goes with this sweater.

   What do I need to know about the hat?

   I want to know _____ hat goes with this _____.

   Noma can't remember _____ book she bought at the store.

   What can't Noma remember?

   Noma can't remember _____ book she bought at the _____.

3. Write the word **which** letter by letter.

while

1. Circle the word **while** in the sentences.

   James likes to do his homework while he watches television.

   I like to listen to music while I run through the park.

   My aunt and uncle will be here in a little while.

2. Write the word **while** five times.

   _____ _____ _____

   _____ _____

3. Unscramble the word. On the line below, write the numbers in order that correspond with the correctly spelled word.

i	h	w	l	e
1	2	3	4	5

   _____

4. Find the word **while** five times.

f	o	w	h	i	l	e	t	w	x	z
w	c	h	w	c	e	m	w	p	g	n
h	o	c	h	l	o	d	h	r	f	c
i	c	l	i	d	o	r	i	b	h	f
l	m	h	l	a	m	n	l	f	y	w
e	w	z	e	z	b	c	e	s	a	w
f	e	c	i	m	h	e	z	f	p	j

Name_____

·· women ··

1. Circle the word **women** in the sentences.

   There are many women singing in the choir.

   Most of my teachers have been women.

   I like to watch the team of women ice skaters.

2. Circle the correct spelling of the word **women.**
   Put an X on the words that are not correct.

wemen	wommen	women	wimmen	women	woman
women	women	wommen	wommin	women	wimenn

   How many correct words did you find? _____

3. How many small words can you make using the letters in **women**?

   _____

   _____

   How many words did you make? _____

4. Use the word **women** in complete sentences to describe the following picture.

   _____

   _____

   _____

   _____

   _____

   _____

   _____

Name_____

1. Circle the word **would** in the sentences.

    Jeff would like you to give him a ride home.
    I would not want to be sick over winter vacation.
    Would you please pass the ice cream?

2. Write the word **would** five times.

    _____   _____   _____

    _____   _____

3. Unscramble the word. On the line below, write the numbers in order that correspond with the correctly spelled word.

    d   w   u   o   l
    1   2   3   4   5

    _____

4. Find the word **would** five times.

w	o	u	l	d	g	o	w	b	y	x
c	m	l	d	w	c	l	o	d	c	w
c	g	h	m	o	d	v	u	v	a	o
e	h	o	t	u	c	g	l	z	q	u
r	h	f	d	l	l	a	d	a	u	l
f	d	c	l	d	z	t	e	s	h	d
b	a	w	o	u	l	d	g	b	c	k

Name_____

..write..

1. Circle the word **write** in the sentences.

   Will you write me a letter when you go to Florida?
   My little brother just learned how to write his name.
   John has to write a long report on South America.

2. Write the word **write** five times.

   _____   _____   _____

   _____   _____

3. Write the word **write** letter by letter.

4. Use the word **write** in complete sentences
   to describe the following picture.

   _____

   _____

   _____

   _____

   _____

your

1. Circle the word **your** in the sentences.

    Be sure to take your vitamin every day.
    Your mother wants you to call home.
    I think I heard your dog barking.

    Hi Mom

2. Write the word **your** five times.

    _____ _____ _____

    _____ _____

3. Fill in the blanks. Use the lifelong word where it is appropriate.

    The teacher said to turn in _____ homework.

    What did the teacher say?

    The _____ said to turn in _____ homework.

    If you want to play, raise _____ hand.

    What should you do if you want to play?

    If you want to _____, raise _____ hand.

    You should brush _____ teeth before bedtime.

    What should you do before bedtime?

    You should brush _____ teeth _____ bedtime.

4. Write the word **your** letter by letter.

    y
    ___
    ___ ___
    ___ ___ ___
    ___ ___ ___ ___

you're

1. Circle the word **you're** in the sentences.

   I think you're really nice.

   Don't go on that roller coaster if you're afraid of heights.

   If you're not too busy tomorrow, come over to my house.

2. Write the word **you're** five times.

   _____   _____   _____

   _____   _____

3. Circle the correct spelling of the word **you're.**
   Put an X on the words that are not correct.

   your   you're   you'r   you'are   you're   you're

   you're   youre   you're   your's   you're   you're

   How many correct words did you find? _____

4. Write the word **you're** letter by letter.

   ___

   ___ ___

   ___ ___ ___

   ___ ___ ___ ___

   ___ ___ ___ ___ ___

   ___ ___ ___ ___ ___ ___

Name

Write On!

Write each lifelong word five times.

1. _____
2. _____
3. _____
4. _____
5. _____

1. _____
2. _____
3. _____
4. _____
5. _____

1. _____
2. _____
3. _____
4. _____
5. _____

1. _____
2. _____
3. _____
4. _____
5. _____

1. _____
2. _____
3. _____
4. _____
5. _____

1. _____
2. _____
3. _____
4. _____
5. _____

Lifelong Words Checklist

Student Name	about	address	again	a lot	although	always	around	because	been	before	birthday	bought	busy	calendar	children	come	coming	could	couldn't	didn't	different	does	doesn't	done
1.																								
2.																								
3.																								
4.																								
5.																								
6.																								
7.																								
8.																								
9.																								
10.																								
11.																								
12.																								
13.																								
14.																								
15.																								
16.																								
17.																								
18.																								
19.																								
20.																								
21.																								
22.																								
23.																								
24.																								
25.																								
26.																								
27.																								
28.																								
29.																								
30.																								

Lifelong Words Checklist
(continued)

Student Name	early	easy	enough	every	everybody	favorite	first	friend	girl	goes	grade	guess	haven't	having	hear	heard	here	hour	house	knew	know	language	many	name	new	none
1.																										
2.																										
3.																										
4.																										
5.																										
6.																										
7.																										
8.																										
9.																										
10.																										
11.																										
12.																										
13.																										
14.																										
15.																										
16.																										
17.																										
18.																										
19.																										
20.																										
21.																										
22.																										
23.																										
24.																										
25.																										
26.																										
27.																										
28.																										
29.																										
30.																										

Lifelong Words Checklist
(continued)

Student Name	often	once	only	our	people	picture	pretty	probably	receive	remember	right	said	school	should	some	something	store	suppose	surprise	taught	teacher	their	there	they're	thought
1.																									
2.																									
3.																									
4.																									
5.																									
6.																									
7.																									
8.																									
9.																									
10.																									
11.																									
12.																									
13.																									
14.																									
15.																									
16.																									
17.																									
18.																									
19.																									
20.																									
21.																									
22.																									
23.																									
24.																									
25.																									
26.																									
27.																									
28.																									
29.																									
30.																									

Student Name	threw	through	to	together	tomorrow	tonight	too	two	until	used	very	way	wear	weigh	we're	were	when	where	which	while	women	would	write	your	you're
1.																									
2.																									
3.																									
4.																									
5.																									
6.																									
7.																									
8.																									
9.																									
10.																									
11.																									
12.																									
13.																									
14.																									
15.																									
16.																									
17.																									
18.																									
19.																									
20.																									
21.																									
22.																									
23.																									
24.																									
25.																									
26.																									
27.																									
28.																									
29.																									
30.																									

Answers

about (page 6)

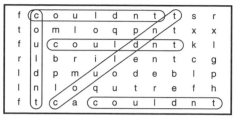

always (page 11)

unscramble: 2 5 3 1 6 4 or
              1 5 3 2 6 4

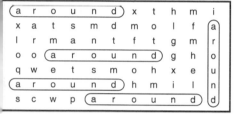

around (page 12)

unscramble: 2 4 3 5 6 1

before (page 15)

unscramble: 6 5 1 4 3 2 or
              6 2 1 4 3 5

calendar (page 19)

unscramble: 6 2 3 8 7 5 1 4 or
              6 1 3 8 7 5 2 4

come (page 21)

unscramble: 4 1 3 2

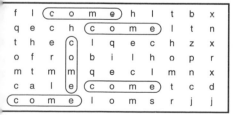

couldn't (page 24)

unscramble: 5 4 7 6 8 2 3

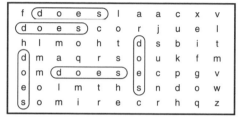

does (page 27)

unscramble: 2 4 3 1

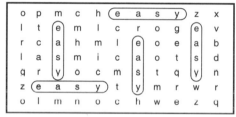

done (page 29)

unscramble: 4 2 3 1

easy (page 31)

unscramble: 4 3 2 1

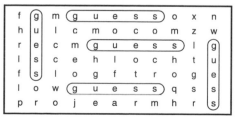

every (page 33)

unscramble: 3 4 2 5 1 or
              2 4 3 5 1

favorite (page 35)

unscramble: 5 4 8 1 7 6 3 2

friend (page 37)

unscramble: 6 1 5 2 4 3

goes (page 39)

unscramble: 3 2 4 1

guess (page 41)

unscramble: 4 3 1 5 2 or
              4 3 1 2 5

having (page 43)

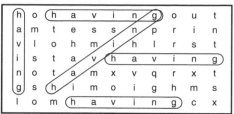

heard (page 45)

unscramble: 4 5 3 1 2

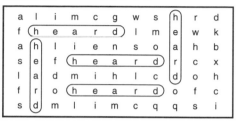

hour (page 47)

unscramble: 3 4 1 2

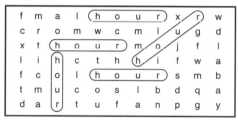

know (page 50)

unscramble: 3 4 2 1

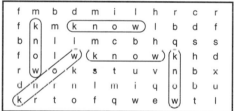

many (page 52)

unscramble: 3 2 4 1

new (page 54)

unscramble: 2 3 1

none (page 55)

unscramble: 2 3 1 4 or
              1 3 2 4

Answers

once (page 57)
unscramble: 3 2 4 1

our (page 59)
unscramble: 2 3 1

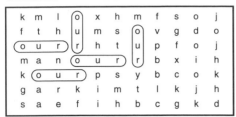

probably (page 63)
unscramble: 1 7 8 4 6 5 2 3 or
1 7 8 5 6 4 2 3

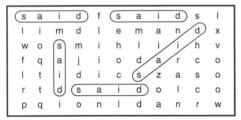

said (page 67)
unscramble: 2 4 3 1

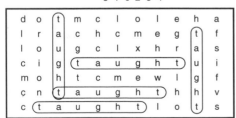

some (page 70)
unscramble: 2 3 1 4

store (page 72)
unscramble: 5 1 4 3 2

surprise (page 74)
unscramble: 7 6 5 4 8 3 2 1 or
2 6 8 4 5 3 7 1

taught (page 75)
unscramble: 4 1 6 2 3 5 or
5 1 6 2 3 4

there (page 78)

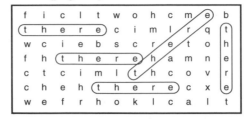

thought (page 80)
unscramble: 2 5 3 4 7 6 1 or
1 6 3 4 7 5 2

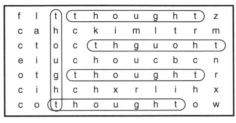

through (page 82)
unscramble: 1 2 6 4 5 7 3 or
1 3 6 4 5 7 2

to (page 83)

tomorrow (page 85)

tonight (page 86)
unscramble: 6 4 5 1 3 7 2 or
2 4 5 1 3 7 6

used (page 90)
unscramble: 4 3 2 1

weigh (page 94)
unscramble: 1 4 5 3 2

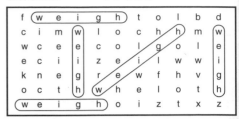

were (page 96)

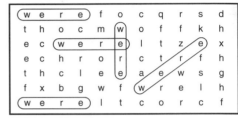

where (page 98)
unscramble: 4 5 3 2 1 or
4 5 1 2 3

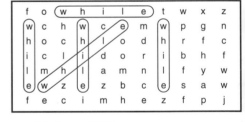

while (page 100)
unscramble: 3 2 1 4 5

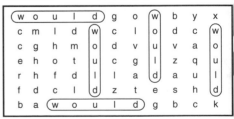

would (page 102)
unscramble: 2 4 3 5 1